YOU CHOOSE
BOOKS

FOUNDING THE
UNITED STATES

FIGHTING FOR
INDEPENDENCE

An Interactive American Revolution Adventure

by Blake Hoena

Consultant:
Richard Bell, PhD
Associate Professor of History
University of Maryland, College Park

CAPSTONE PRESS
a capstone imprint

You Choose Books are published by Capstone Press,
1710 Roe Crest Drive, North Mankato, Minnesota 56003
www.mycapstone.com

Library of Congress Cataloging-in-Publication Data
Library of Congress Cataloging-in-Publication data is available on the Library of
Congress website.

978-1-5435-1540-4 (library binding)
978-1-5435-1547-3 (paperback)

Editorial Credits
Adrian Vigliano, editor; Bobbie Nuytten, designer;
Kelly Garvin, media researcher; Kathy McColley, production specialist

Photo Credits
Alamy: nsf, 46, World History Archive, 41; Bridgeman Images/Troiani, Don
(b.1949)/Private Collection, cover; Capstone Press, 76; Getty Images/Fine Art/
Contributor, 35; North Wind Picture Archive, 6, 16, 24, 45, 56, 67, 81, 89, 92, 98,
100, 104; Shutterstock/Everett Historical, 70

Artistic elements: Shutterstock: Abstractor, photka

Printed and bound in Canada.
PA020

Table of Contents

ABOUT YOUR ADVENTURE

YOU are about to enter the Revolutionary War. The American colonies have declared their independence from Great Britain. Now they have to fight one of the world's most powerful armies. Battles will be won and lost in both the northern and southern colonies. Any one of them could decide the fate of the Continental Army.

In this book you'll explore how the choices people made meant the difference between life and death. The events you'll experience happened to real people.

Chapter One sets the scene. Then you choose which path to read. Follow the directions at the bottom of each page. The choices you make will change your outcome. After you finish your path, go back and read the others for new perspectives and more adventures.

YOU CHOOSE the path
you take through history.

Paul Revere's ride on April 18, 1775, became a famous story of the American Revolution.

SHOT HEARD AROUND THE WORLD

It is the night of April 18, 1775. A man in a dark overcoat sneaks along Boston's waterfront. Behind him two lanterns hang from Christ Church's bell tower. They shine like beacons. The man reaches the North End, a neighborhood along the Charles River. Two sailors step out of the shadows to greet him.

"Is that you, Paul?" one of them asks.

"Aye," Paul Revere replies. "We best hurry across."

"Our boat's over here," the other man says.

The three men board a small rowboat. The two sailors pull on the oars while Revere watches a British warship. It looms large in the night but they slip safely past.

Turn the page.

On the other side of the river, members of the Sons of Liberty meet Revere. Led by Samuel Adams, John Hancock, and others, this secret organization has fought to protect colonists' rights.

"We saw the signal," one of the men says.

"Then you know I must warn Adams and Hancock," Revere says. "The British are on the move."

"Take my mount," the man says, offering his horse. Revere gets on the horse and then he is off.

For years some colonists have been at odds with British rule. The British Parliament imposed taxes many believe are unfair and passed laws to govern the colonies. The relationship between the colonists and the British has grown especially tense in Boston. In 1770 British soldiers fired on a crowd of colonists, killing five. This event came to be known as the Boston Massacre.

Three years later came the Boston Tea Party, in which colonists dumped tea into Boston Harbor to protest British taxes. After this, Parliament declared Massachusetts to be in a state of rebellion. Thousands of British soldiers were stationed in and around Boston.

General Thomas Gage, leader of the British forces in Boston, heard that the colonists had been arming themselves. Gage was informed that militia groups had stashed weapons in Concord. So on the night of April 18, Gage ordered several hundred British soldiers to destroy the colonists' arms and arrest Adams and Hancock.

The lanterns Revere saw hanging from the church tower were part of a warning system set up by the Sons of Liberty. The two lanterns told him that British troops would leave Boston by sailing across the Charles River. One lantern would have meant the British were planning to leave by land.

Turn the page.

As he rides Revere warns everyone he sees. "The British are coming!" he tells town leaders. "Prepare yourselves," he calls out to members of the militia. Colonists begin to arm themselves.

Shortly after midnight Revere reaches the house where Adams and Hancock are staying.

"It's late. Keep quiet," a guard says, blocking Revere's way. But he is determined to have his warning heard.

"Noise! You'll have noise," Revere shouts. "The regulars are coming!"

A moment later Hancock pokes his head out of a window. "What's all the racket?" he asks, and then he sees who is shouting. "Oh, you, Revere. Come in. Come in."

Another rider arrives as Revere sits down with Hancock and Adams.

"Ah, it's William Dawes," Hancock says when the man barges into the room. Dawes has also been sent from Boston to warn of the approaching British soldiers.

"You and Paul must continue on to Concord," Adams tells them. "We need to make sure the weapons are safe."

After a quick meal, Revere and Dawes mount their horses and ride into the night. Before reaching Concord, the pair comes across Samuel Prescott, another member of the Sons of Liberty.

"I grew up in Concord," he tells them. "Let me lead the way."

As they ride through the morning, they run into a British patrol.

"You three, halt!" orders the British commander.

Turn the page.

"Scatter!" Prescott shouts. The three riders split up, and the British give chase. Dawes escapes to a nearby farmhouse. But he is thrown from his horse and injured. He cannot continue on to Concord. Revere does not get very far and is captured. The British question him and take his horse before letting him go. He returns to Lexington on foot. But Prescott evades the British soldiers. The thud of hoofbeats echoes through the night.

"Ya! Ya!" Prescott shouts at his horse. It jumps over a stone wall, landing loudly on the other side.

The British halt their horses. Stopping at the wall, they watch Prescott disappear into the night.

Prescott continues on to Concord and warns the colonists of the British approach. At daybreak on April 19 several hundred British soldiers march into Lexington. Just under a hundred armed patriots have gathered in town. The two groups face each other, neither sure of what to do.

"Lay down your weapons," one of the British officers orders.

Then a shot rings out. No one knows who fired it, but soon the British unload their muskets as the patriots flee. When the smoke clears, several colonists are dead.

The British march on to Concord. There, some soldiers are ordered to guard the road leading into town, including the North Bridge. The rest burst into people's homes and barns looking for weapons.

Meanwhile, hundreds of patriot militia members gather north of town. They are mostly shop owners and farmers. But these colonists have been readying themselves for the moment when they would need to stand up to the British. They march toward the North Bridge.

Turn the page.

"Halt!" a British soldier commands.

The militia fire their muskets. It marks the moment the patriots openly begin to fight for their freedom from British rule. More shots ring out as the militia marches into town.

"Fall back! Fall back!" the British commander calls out. "To Lexington!"

The British flee from Concord, but the militia harass them on their retreat. Patriots hide behind trees and fire at the British soldiers. They duck behind stone walls and unload their muskets. When the British reach Lexington, reinforcements meet them. But the militia's numbers have grown to nearly 2,000. The British are heavily outnumbered.

"To Boston," the British commander orders.

Musket balls whiz through the night.
The British continue their retreat. They are
harried all the way back to Boston. They suffer
nearly 300 casualties in the first fighting of the
American Revolution.

Though the battles at Lexington and
Concord are victories for the patriots, there is
much more fighting ahead. Many more battles
will be fought before the war for independence
can be won. How will you help the patriots in
their fight for freedom?

To join the Continental Army in defending the
northern colonies, turn to page 17.

To help seek an alliance with a foreign
government, turn to page 47.

To defend the southern colonies as a member of
the militia, turn to page 71.

The first shot fired on Lexington Common on April 19, 1775, is often referred to as the "shot heard around the world."

CHAPTER 2

THE BEGINNINGS OF WAR

On April 19, 1775, the first shots of the American Revolution are fired at the Battles of Lexington and Concord northwest of Boston. You are among the thousands of militia fighters who drive the Redcoats across the Charles River and back to Boston.

Because of your military experience in the French and Indian War, you receive an officer's commission in the colonial army. You are placed in command of a small group of soldiers.

17

General Artemis Ward takes charge of the growing forces surrounding Boston. You are surprised by the number of colonists willing to take up arms against the British.

Turn the page.

The patriots easily outnumber the Redcoats defending the city, but your supplies are low.

"We have neither the weapons nor the ammunition to take the city," Ward tells his officers.

Colonel Benedict Arnold knows of several cannons at Fort Ticonderoga. The British control this fort in northeastern New York.

"It is poorly defended," Arnold says. "And those cannons could help us drive the British from Boston."

How will you help in the fighting?

To join Ward in the siege of Boston, go to page 19.

To join Arnold in attacking British forces at Fort Ticonderoga, turn to page 21.

As colonial forces surround Boston, your numbers swell. But the militia members are a ragtag bunch. The Redcoats are professional soldiers. Even if your forces had enough weapons, you would be hard-pressed to drive the British from Boston.

Instead of attacking, Ward commands the men to dig in. You help build fortifications in the hills overlooking Boston and its harbor.

While you work, the Second Continental Congress is established. This group of lawmakers meets in Philadelphia, which becomes the colonial capital. The Second Continental Congress will govern the colonies during the war. You and your men are now part of the Continental Army.

The siege of Boston continues throughout the spring. In mid-June General Ward receives news that the British are planning an attack. He meets with his officers to discuss plans.

Turn the page.

"They hope to secure the Charlestown Peninsula," he tells his officers as he points to a map of the area.

"That will give them better control of the harbor," one officer says, studying the map.

"We won't be able to stop them from receiving reinforcements and supplies," another adds.

"Congress will select a leader for the army soon," a third officer says. "We should wait until he arrives. Maybe he'll bring supplies."

"But we can't just retreat from the peninsula," another officer argues. "We should make the Redcoats earn any ground they capture."

Ward turns to you. "What would you recommend?" he asks.

To suggest a defense of the Charlestown Peninsula, turn to page 23.

To let the British capture the Charlestown Peninsula, turn to page 34.

20

The forces laying siege to Boston need artillery to drive the British out of the city. So you and your men join Colonel Arnold in his plans to attack British forces at Fort Ticonderoga.

You spend the next couple of days recruiting help for the attack. Colonel Ethan Allen joins you. He and Arnold gather a force of more than 150 men.

Then you head out. On the night of May 9 you reach Lake Champlain. The fort is on the opposite shore.

Shortly after midnight boats arrive to carry you across. But there are not enough for all of the men.

Allen and Arnold order half of your force to board the boats. You join them.

Turn the page.

"We'll send the boats back," Arnold tells the remaining soldiers.

It is nearing daybreak when you reach the opposite shore.

"It will be hours before the boats return with the rest of the men," Allen says. "If we wait we will lose the element of surprise."

"But if we attack now, we won't have the advantage of numbers," Arnold argues.

"Could I make a suggestion?" you ask.

The two commanders turn to you.

To suggest attacking now, turn to page 25.

To recommend waiting, turn to page 37.

"We cannot give the British complete control of Boston Harbor," you say.

General Ward agrees. He orders Colonel William Prescott to fortify Bunker Hill on the northwest side of the Charlestown Peninsula. You and your men join him.

On the night of June 16 you sneak onto the peninsula. From Bunker Hill you can see the lights of Boston across the Charles River. Between you and the city, several warships patrol the river. You hope the British will not notice your preparations.

Before you lift the first shovelful of dirt, Prescott and his officers begin to argue over plans.

"Bunker Hill is too far back from the shore," one officer says. "We should move our forces up to Breed's Hill."

23

Turn the page.

Fortifying a position was an important part of preparing for battle during the Revolutionary War.

"But this is where General Ward commanded us to set up our fortifications," another officer argues. "We can't disobey orders."

"Well we can't spend all night arguing," you pipe in.

Prescott turns to you and asks, "Then what would you have us do?"

To suggest defending Breed's Hill, turn to page 26.

To continue preparing to defend Bunker Hill, turn to page 39.

"We won't need numbers to force our way in," you say, "not if we take the fort by surprise."

The commanders consider your words and then both men nod in agreement. Before long, you are sneaking through the woods by the growing light. When you get near the fort, you see it is rundown and ill-prepared for an attack.

"I see only one sentry," you whisper. Then you charge out of your hiding spot.

BANG! A musket ball whizzes through the night. But no one is injured. A moment later your men are inside the fort. You have weapons aimed at the British soldiers before they can even prepare to fight back. They surrender. The fort is yours!

That winter you help move the fort's cannons to the colonial troops besieging Boston.

25

Turn to page 29.

"Breed's Hill would give us a better view of the harbor," you say. "We'll be able to see the British approach."

Prescott orders the men to build fortifications around Breed's Hill. You and your men dig in. You move shovel after shovel of dirt. By the time the sunrise colors the horizon, you are finished. You have built a dirt wall more than 100 feet long and 6 feet high around the hill.

BOOM! One of the British warships fires. You duck behind your fortifications. More warships fire. Cannonballs thud around you, but your defenses hold. As British troops land on the eastern side of the peninsula, Prescott calls for reinforcements.

Early that afternoon the British begin their march on Breed's Hill. You hear someone call out, "Hold your fire until you see the whites of their eyes."

You aim. The British charge, making a rush up the hill. When they are close, you fire.

You see Redcoats drop. You quickly reload your musket and let loose another volley. More Redcoats fall.

"Fall back," the British officers order.

A cheer goes up among your men. Your defenses are holding. But the British re-form their battle lines. The attack is not over.

They charge again. Again you fire your musket. Shots ring out. Redcoats fall dead or dying. Again the British officers call for a retreat. This time, there is little cheering among your army. You are low on ammunition.

As the Redcoats make their next charge, your forces unload their muskets again. The British casualties are heavy. But your line falters as the ammunition runs out.

Turn the page.

The British charge up the hill, bayonets at the ready. They cut through your defenses.

You hear voices shouting, "Fall back!" But this time the order comes from the officers on your side.

You begin your retreat. The British charge. Colonials fall.

The battle is lost, but not the war. Although you are forced from the Charlestown Peninsula, the British suffer more than 1,000 casualties during the Battle of Bunker Hill. The Continental Army proved it could put up a fight against the well-trained British Army.

28

Go to page 29.

In July 1775 General George Washington takes command of the forces surrounding Boston. Though the British had taken control of the Charlestown Peninsula, they did not have the men to break the siege of Boston. Meanwhile, the Continental Army did not have the weapons to force the British from the city. So the two sides are at a stalemate.

That fall Washington orders the cannons captured at Fort Ticonderoga to be brought to Boston. They arrive in the spring of 1776.

With the cannons, the Continental Army forces the British from Boston. They sail to Halifax in the British colony of Nova Scotia. Afterward, you join Washington and the Continental Army on the way to New York City.

Turn the page.

"That's where I believe the British will attack next," Washington says. "If they take the city, they will separate New England from the rest of the colonies."

You arrive in New York in April 1776. In June you learn that the British are sailing to New York City.

Then in July news reaches you that the Declaration of Independence has been signed. The Declaration states that the American colonies are now an independent nation. Now, you need to win that freedom from the British.

In August the British land on Staten Island, New York, with hundreds of ships and thousands of troops. Washington learns that they plan to attack Long Island. He moves half his army there to set up fortifications in Brooklyn Heights.

When the British move a large force onto Long Island, you go to meet them in battle. Both sides suffer heavy casualties, and you are forced to retreat to your fortifications in Brooklyn Heights. Behind you is the East River and in front of you is the British Army.

Washington meets with his officers to decide the Continental Army's next move.

"The British outnumber us," one officer says.

"But if we can't hold this position, they could take New York City," another officer argues.

"Do you have any thoughts on our situation?" Washington asks you.

31

To tell him to retreat, turn to page 32.

To suggest holding your ground, turn to page 42.

"If we stay and fight, the British could sail up the East River," you say. "We would be surrounded."

"Then they would force our surrender, and the war would be lost," Washington replies. "We need to retreat to Manhattan Island."

Washington orders the retreat. Under the cover of night, your forces slip across the East River and onto Manhattan Island.

Over the next few weeks and months, Washington leads the Continental Army on a strategic retreat. You march north to Harlem Heights. After a short skirmish there, you flee again to evade capture.

The Continental Army continues to suffer further defeats. In October you lose the Battle of White Plains. In November Continental troops are driven from Fort Washington.

Eventually you cross the Hudson River into New Jersey. You have lost New York. But worse, British forces push you south across the Delaware River and into Pennsylvania.

As winter sets in, morale is low and you have lost thousands of troops. The Continental Army is in need of food and clothing. Many soldiers are sick. Even Washington is on the verge of thinking that the war is lost.

"We should continue our retreat," one of Washington's officers suggests.

"What we need is a victory to boost morale," another officer argues.

"Can I make a suggestion?" you ask.

Washington turns to you and nods.

To argue for marching south, turn to page 43.

To recommend attacking the British, turn to page 44.

33

"It's best to wait until the new commander of the Continental Army arrives," you say.

Several of the other officers raise their voices in disagreement. "We cannot let the British have complete control of the harbor," one argues.

Another adds, "If we do, they could easily bring more troops and weapons into the city."

"We wouldn't have the numbers to stop them then," Ward says. "And why have we gathered our forces here if not to give the British a fight?"

On June 16 General Ward orders Colonel Prescott to set up fortifications on Bunker Hill. But instead Prescott sets up his defense on Breed's Hill, partially because of its more central location on Charlestown Peninsula.

The next morning you wake to the *BOOM! BOOM! BOOM!* of British cannons. Their warships fire on Prescott's fortifications.

The Battle of Bunker Hill resulted in significant casualties for both armies.

Later in the day, you watch as British troops land on the peninsula.

The fight is fierce. The British attack, but Prescott's defenses drive them back. Again the British attack. And again Prescott's defenses hold. On the third charge, you hear the Continental Army's musket fire falter.

"They must be running out of ammunition," says an officer standing next to you.

Turn the page.

35

You watch in horror as the British charge up the fortification. Hand-to-hand combat begins as the British attack with bayonets.

Prescott calls for a retreat. Though the battle is lost and the Continental Army is driven from the peninsula, its soldiers fought well. They proved that they could stand against the well-trained Redcoats.

Even though your recommendation would have prevented the loss of lives, it would not have helped boost the troops' morale. Your suggestion also must have caused General Ward to lose confidence in you. You continue to serve the general. But it is clear you will no longer help decide the Continental Army's course of action during the war.

36

THE END
To follow another path, turn to page 15.
To read the conclusion, turn to page 101.

"Let's wait for the remainder of our men," you say.

Arnold frowns at that suggestion. "I don't know. They will see us coming once the sun is up."

"I have a plan," Allen says.

Allen has you stay behind to wait for the rest of the men while he and Arnold scout out the fort. They will only attack if they feel they can easily capture it.

An hour passes. The boats with the rest of your men have not returned. Then in the distance you hear a musket shot. Moments later, there is cheering. When you finally arrive at the fort with the rest of the men, Arnold and Allen have already captured it.

That winter Arnold is ordered to bring the cannons to Boston to help in the siege.

Turn the page.

37

"You will stay behind to defend the fort," he orders.

You spend the next year helping to rebuild and strengthen the fort. You hear that the British have been forced from Boston and that the fighting has moved to New York City.

You do not see any fighting again until the summer of 1777. A large force of British soldiers marches on the fort. Your commanding officer, General Arthur St. Claire, decides to retreat without a fight.

This decision angers many in Congress. General St. Claire is court-martialed for abandoning the fort. You also suffer from the disgrace and lose your commission as an officer. Your days as a soldier are over.

THE END

To follow another path, turn to page 15.
To read the conclusion, turn to page 101.

"We must follow Ward's orders," you say.

Prescott continues to review the situation as you and the other officers around him argue.

"I think if General Ward were here, he would see that Breed's Hill is better suited for our defense," Prescott decides.

He orders the men to build fortifications around Breed's Hill. You and your men start to dig in. By the next morning, you have created a 6-foot-tall dirt wall surrounding the hill.

BOOM! A British warship fires on your fortifications. Your work ends as you duck behind the wall you built. More ships open fire. Cannonballs pound your fortifications, thudding against the walls. But your defenses hold. Early that afternoon the British march on Breed's Hill. You hear someone call out, "Hold your fire until you see the whites of their eyes!"

Turn the page.

You aim as the British rush up the hill. When they are close, you fire. Redcoats drop. You reload and let loose another volley.

"Retreat!" the British commander orders. Once they re-form their line, the British attack again. Again you drive them back.

Throughout your ranks you hear soldiers say that they are low on ammunition. Then the British charge again. You fire your musket into their line. But when you reach into your cartridge box, you find it empty. You glance around. Others have also stopped firing.

Looking up you see charging Redcoats climbing over your fortifications. You try to hold them back, but they are armed with bayonets on the ends of their muskets. They cut through your defenses. Continental soldiers fall.

Most of the fighting at the Battle of Bunker Hill took place on nearby Breed's Hill.

You hear the call to retreat, but as you turn to flee, you collide with a British soldier. You feel a sharp sting and look down to see the Redcoat's blade stuck between your ribs. You fall to the ground, dying, as the British pursue the retreating colonial troops.

THE END

To follow another path, turn to page 15.
To read the conclusion, turn to page 101.

The weather is bad, so you cannot see what is happening beyond your fortifications. But you know that the weather also makes it difficult for the British and prevents them from attacking.

"We have to hold our ground," you say.

"I cannot risk it," Washington says. "If we do not retreat now, the British could surround us and force our surrender. We will make the safe choice and fight another day."

All night soldiers march down to the ferry. They cross the East River onto Manhattan Island. Not a single solider is lost in the effort. But Washington has lost respect for your decisions. He no longer feels you will make the right choices. You continue your fight for the Continental Army. But you are no longer in a position to advise Washington on his decisions.

42

THE END

To follow another path, turn to page 15.
To read the conclusion, turn to page 101.

"We could regroup our forces at Philadelphia," you say.

As his officers argue over their desperate situation, Washington sits back in his chair to think. After several moments he says, "It is not time to retreat. It is time we take the fight to the British."

But you do not take part in the fight. He sends you to defend Philadelphia. While there you hear of Washington's successes at battles in Trenton and Princeton. You wish you could have been there.

In 1777 the British march on Philadelphia. Washington tries to stop them, but his army is defeated at the Battle of Brandywine. As the fighting takes place, you help the members of the Second Continental Congress flee. The British take control of Philadelphia in September. But Congress is safe. The patriots can continue to fight.

43

THE END

To follow another path, turn to page 15.
To read the conclusion, turn to page 101.

"It is not time to retreat," you argue. "We need to take the fight to the British."

Washington agrees. Soon you learn of a force of Hessians setting up its winter camp across the river in Trenton, New Jersey. The British hired these German soldiers to bolster their forces.

Washington sees this as a chance for a much-needed victory. On Christmas night he decides to cross the Delaware River and attack the Hessians by surprise. The crossing is dangerous. The weather is frigid and the water is icy. To fall overboard would mean certain death.

Your forces land north of Trenton. Then you march through the morning to Trenton. The Hessians do not suspect an attack, so you catch them by surprise. You take the enemy troops prisoner and score a decisive victory.

Washington's forces used a variety of ferries and cargo boats to bring 18 cannons across the Delaware River.

Just when you thought you were on the verge of losing the war, you have breathed new life into the patriots' fight for freedom. The victory at the Battle of Trenton emboldens the patriots.

Shortly afterward, the Continental Army scores another victory at the Battle of Princeton, pushing British forces out of New Jersey.

You have turned the tide of the war in favor of the patriots.

THE END

To follow another path, turn to page 15.
To read the conclusion, turn to page 101.

The first meeting of the Second Continental Congress only had delegates from 12 of the 13 colonies. Georgia was the final colony to send delegates in July 1775.

CHAPTER 3

A NEEDED ALLIANCE

Soon after the start of the Revolutionary War, the Second Continental Congress meets. This group of colonial lawmakers makes your home of Philadelphia, Pennsylvania, its capital. These men will govern the colonies during the Revolution.

The Continental Congress has several goals. One is to form a Continental Army out of the colonial militia. In June 1775 lawmakers name General George Washington commander.

Congress also seeks to raise money for the war effort and to gain foreign aid. The Committee of "Secret" Correspondence is tasked with the job of seeking an alliance with other countries. Later it is renamed the Committee of Foreign Affairs.

Turn the page.

Much of the initial fighting breaks out far north, around Boston, Massachusetts. Instead of enlisting in the army, you seek to be an aide to one of the delegates in Congress. The decisions it makes will affect the war's outcome just as much as the military successes. You are educated, fluent in French, and know that France is one of the colonies' most likely allies. Great Britain and France have often been in conflict over the years. In the French and Indian War, France lost territory in North America to the British.

Soon you are presented with an opportunity to work for one of two important figures. Who will you help in seeking support for the patriots?

48

To join Benjamin Franklin in seeking an alliance, go to page 49.

To join the Marquis de Lafayette in supporting the patriots, turn to page 51.

Benjamin Franklin is a scientist and journalist. Some of his major achievements were establishing the idea of public libraries and inventing bifocals. He is also an important political figure in Pennsylvania.

When fighting begins, he is chosen to represent Pennsylvania in the Second Continental Congress. He is given several important jobs, including being a key member of the Committee of "Secret" Correspondence.

You are excited to be working with this important member of the new government.

"We have a difficult task ahead of us," he says. "I'm not sure anyone is willing to help our desperate cause."

"But, sir, you have traveled throughout Europe," you tell Franklin. "You have many contacts overseas."

Turn the page.

"Aye, it is true," he replies with a laugh. "I have even met King Louis XV of France. Perhaps he will hear us out."

Toward the end of 1775 French officials reach out to Franklin. At the time the Continental Army is laying siege to British forces controlling Boston.

"We need to gain control of the city soon," you say, "but our army doesn't have the needed weapons."

"The French could provide support," Franklin says. "But I am not sure if they would risk aiding a British colony."

You and Franklin discuss what should be done. Which side of the argument do you take?

To suggest that Congress declare independence from Great Britain, turn to page 53.

To suggest asking for immediate aid from the French, turn to page 62.

In 1776 you and Captain Marquis de Lafayette hear of negotiations between the French and the newly formed United States of America. No official agreements have been signed. But French officers are being sent to America to help in the fight against British rule. You are assigned to be Captain Lafayette's American aide.

He arrives in the United States in the spring of 1777. That summer you and Lafayette meet General George Washington, leader of the Continental Army. He invites Lafayette to inspect his troops. You watch as the two commanders quickly become friends.

Lafayette is given an honorary commission of major general in the Continental Army. You and Lafayette join Washington's forces. You see your first action that fall at the Battle of Brandywine. You fight on horseback alongside Lafayette. During intense fighting you hear him scream in pain.

Turn the page.

"I've been shot," he moans.

You see blood staining his uniform. All around you, colonial forces flee from the British advance.

"We should pull back," you say.

"We need to rally the troops," he says. Lafayette rides back and forth across the battlefield. "Form up! Form up!" he shouts.

Despite his injury, Lafayette helps keep order on the battlefield. General Washington is impressed. He recommends that Lafayette receive his own command. That winter Lafayette is asked to lead an invasion of Britain's Canadian colonies.

"It's a great honor," you say. But you also know that Lafayette will miss fighting by Washington's side.

"What should I do?" he asks.

To advise him to stay with Washington, turn to page 55.

To urge him to take the command of the invasion force, turn to page 63.

"I doubt the French or any country will help us," you say. "Not when we are still one of Great Britain's colonies."

"Then we need to declare ourselves an independent nation," Franklin says.

He takes this idea to the Congress. With Franklin's help Thomas Jefferson is given the task of writing a declaration of independence. This document is meant to sever political ties with Great Britain. It will also state that the colonies are now an independent nation known as the United States of America. Congress approves the Declaration of Independence on July 4, 1776.

53

Before long it is time for you to leave with Franklin. You sail to Paris, the French capital, to work on an alliance. Along with declaring your independence you have other good news to share. The Continental Army forced the British out of Boston in the spring of 1776.

Turn the page.

"I am impressed with this news," French foreign minister Comte de Vergennes tells you. "Perhaps the French can aid in your war for independence."

But while you are discussing the details of an alliance with France, you receive bad news.

"Washington is on the run," you tell Franklin. "He lost New York to the British."

The French foreign minister also hears this news. "Perhaps the war is already lost," he says. "It would be risky for my country to openly support a rebellion."

Franklin turns to you for support. You know that the colonies need help or they will not be able to continue the fight for long. What do you recommend to Franklin?

To ask for a secret alliance with France, turn to page 57.

To seek an alliance with Spain instead, turn to page 60.

"I am not sure about this command," you tell Lafayette. "The colonists already failed once to invade Britain's Canadian colonies. It would be better to stay with Washington at Valley Forge."

Lafayette agrees and says with a laugh, "Can you imagine invading the Canadian colonies in the middle of winter?"

You stay at Valley Forge with Washington and the Continental Army. It turns out to be a miserable winter. Soldiers lack proper clothing. Supplies of food run low. The troops suffer. Many die from the cold and starvation, and many others desert.

Then in March 1778 you receive word that a treaty between the United States and France has been signed. This helps boost morale among the Continental Army soldiers. Soon French forces will be arriving to bolster their forces.

Turn the page.

Though the French aid helps the American cause, Lafayette worries it is not enough. In 1779 you accompany Lafayette to France. There you work to gain further support for the patriot war effort.

The troops and supplies that Lafayette helps raise come at a crucial time for the Continental Army. You know the patriot war effort has been faltering. Finally the work is done. It is time to return to America to rejoin Washington.

Turn to page 58.

"Perhaps for now the French can provide aid without an official alliance," you whisper.

Franklin proposes this idea to the French minister, and with a sly smile, he agrees.

Supporting the American patriots is popular among the French. But French officials are still wary of an alliance. It would put them in direct conflict with Great Britain. The French want to be sure that the patriots have a chance to defeat the British.

In December 1777 the Continental Army wins the Battle of Saratoga. This gives the French the assurance they need. On February 6, 1778, two treaties are signed. The French offer military aid to the United States in the Treaty of Alliance. The Treaty of Amity and Commerce establishes trade between the new allies.

In 1780 Franklin sends you home. You join General Washington and help in any way you can.

Turn to page 58.

Since the treaty was signed with France, the French have supported the patriots' cause. They have sent troops and arms to help battle the British. That does not mean victory has been easy for the patriots. They have suffered several devastating defeats. But they have also won many important battles.

In the summer of 1781 you are with Washington as he is planning to attack British forces in New York City. Earlier in the war, the Continental Army had been forced from the city. But Washington is hoping that he can retake the city with the aid of several thousand French troops.

As you help with preparations, news arrives of a French fleet heading to Virginia. It is headed toward Yorktown, where British General Charles Cornwallis has his main force stationed.

"We should join forces with the French," one of Washington's officers says. "If we can defeat the main British Army, we could end the war."

"But most of the British troops have withdrawn to Yorktown," another officer argues. "We could easily retake New York."

"What is your advice?" Washington asks, turning to you.

59

To recommend attacking the British at Yorktown, turn to page 65.

To push for attacking the British in New York City, turn to page 68.

"Spain is also an enemy of Great Britain," you say. Spain fought with France against Great Britain in the Seven Years' War. You hope it might now support your cause. "We should seek an alliance."

"Go and make preparations for our departure," Franklin says, after thinking for several minutes.

You leave the room, but Franklin stays behind. You do not see him again until later that night. He does not tell you what he has been doing or hint at any further conversations with the French minister.

"We will leave for Spain tomorrow," he says.

When you arrive in Spain you join Franklin in the meeting with the Spanish foreign minister.

"How has your war for independence been going?" the Spanish minister asks.

"I have received good news," Franklin says. He begins to speak of the Continental Army's recent victories at the Battles of Trenton and Princeton.

"Maybe we could provide you with aid," the minister says. "But we require something in return."

The minister explains that Spain wants to regain territory in North America. Florida was once a Spanish colony. You know that Congress will not agree to those terms. But Franklin does not seem overly worried. Later, he sends you home to tell Congress of Spain's request.

Franklin later returns to Paris and serves as French ambassador during the war. You learn that Franklin convinced France to secretly aid the United States until a formal alliance could be formed.

You do not see Franklin again until he returns home after the war. You are happy to see the United States win freedom from the British. But you will always wonder what role you might have played if you had given Franklin different advice.

THE END

To follow another path, turn to page 15.
To read the conclusion, turn to page 101.

"We should ask the French for help," you say, "before the British break the siege at Boston."

"Let me think about it," Franklin says. "I'll need to discuss any decisions with Congress first."

Franklin does not tell you that he strongly disagrees with your suggestion. The colonies do need aid. But right now other countries do not see the colonies as independent. They see them as belonging to Great Britain. Franklin knows that France will not risk aiding another country's colonies in a fight for independence.

62 Franklin recommends that Congress declare its independence before asking for aid. Congress signs the Declaration of Independence on July 4, 1776. But because of your shortsighted advice, Franklin does not to take you with him when he sails to France to seek an alliance.

THE END

To follow another path, turn to page 15.
To read the conclusion, turn to page 101.

"If you can lead a successful invasion, the Americans could take control of Britain's Canadian colonies," you say.

"It would provide a great service to your countrymen," Lafayette says, nodding.

He decides to take the command. Soon you and Lafayette travel north to make your preparations. But it doesn't take long before you begin to doubt the mission. The force that has been gathered for Lafayette to command is ill-equipped and not very large.

Still you insist that he complete the mission. You think about the previous time when patriots had marched on Quebec and been turned back.

"We will succeed where they failed," you say boldly.

But it is clear that Lafayette has doubts. "I am going to rejoin Washington," he says.

Turn the page.

"But what will I do?" you ask. "We are in the middle of preparing our invasion."

"Then continue without me," he says.

And that is exactly what you do. You keep planning for the attack on Quebec. But as you soon learn, Lafayette was correct in doubting the mission. The Continental Congress withholds funding for the attack and you are never able to march.

Meanwhile, you hear news of Lafayette and his efforts to help the patriots win the war. He goes on to have a great effect on the success of the Continental Army. You, on the other hand, head back to Philadelphia disgraced after your support of a hopeless cause.

THE END
To follow another path, turn to page 15.
To read the conclusion, turn to page 101.

"If we join the French forces sailing to Virginia," you say, "we could surround the British at Yorktown."

"That just might force the British to surrender," Washington adds.

So Washington turns his sights from New York City to Yorktown. The army begins the march to Virginia. You arrive in September.

The combined Continental and French forces nearly double the number of British at Yorktown. But the British are prepared for an attack. Around the town the British have set up a series of small forts armed with cannons.

Washington orders his troops to surround the town. They set up camp outside the range of the British cannons. Meanwhile, French warships take control of the harbor, blocking a British retreat.

On September 29 Washington moves his artillery within range of the town's outer defenses. The British begin firing. The booming of their cannons is deafening. You feel the earth shake as cannonballs thud into the ground. Your forces return fire. You see puffs of dirt kick up whenever a cannonball strikes the British defenses.

The two sides bombard each other for days. Slowly your forces move their artillery forward. They blast the forts defending the town, weakening the British defenses. By October 14 the British have abandoned all but two of the forts protecting the town.

That night Washington orders an attack. While cannon fire rocks the British defenses, you and hundreds of soldiers march forward. Musket balls scream through the air. You return fire. Redcoats take cover.

General Washington (center) and French General Rochambeau (left) joined forces at the Siege of Yorktown.

Eventually you rush over the British defenses. Redcoats fall before your charge as your numbers overwhelm them. By the end of the day, you have captured the last of the forts protecting the town.

Three days later General Cornwallis requests to surrender to General Washington. Then on October 19 both sides officially agree to terms of the British surrender.

THE END

To follow another path, turn to page 15.
To read the conclusion, turn to page 101.

"If we retake New York," you say, "we will have control of all the northern states."

Since early in the war the British have had control of New York City. This has cut off New England from the rest of the country. So Washington likes the idea of moving on the city, especially since he suffered some of his worst defeats there. But still he has his doubts.

"We cannot pass up this opportunity," he says after considering your suggestion. "We have a chance to end the war."

Washington cannot resist the chance of taking back New York and the area north of it from the British. So he sends you north with a small force of men. He takes the majority of his forces and heads for Yorktown.

While you march on New York City, Washington joins forces with the French. Your hope is that you will be able to end the war by retaking the city. But the most important action turns out to be at Yorktown. Washington lays siege to Yorktown, eventually forcing the British to surrender.

The war ends, but you cannot help feeling disappointed to have missed the final battle.

THE END

To follow another path, turn to page 15.
To read the conclusion, turn to page 101.

After several days of debate, the Continental Congress officially adopted the Declaration of Independence on July 4, 1776.

CHAPTER 4

LOYALISTS VERSUS PATRIOTS

Colonists are divided about the Revolutionary War. Many do not know whether they want to be part of an independent nation or stay under British rule. They remain undecided even after the first shots are fired.

Colonists who fight for independence are called patriots. They include the Sons of Liberty. Colonists who support Great Britain are called loyalists.

Loyalists think their lives will be better off under British rule. They reason that the colonies need British protection and that British trade is too important to lose.

Turn the page.

On July 4, 1776, Congress officially adopts the Declaration of Independence. This document states that the colonies are now a group of independent states united in their fight against British rule. At the time, you served in the militia of your home state of Georgia. Colonists were moving west, and you helped protect them. For the Revolutionary War, your previous military experience earns you an officer's commission in the Continental Army. You are then assigned to defend Savannah, Georgia.

In the fall of 1777 the Continental Army defeats the British at the Battle of Saratoga, helping to seal an alliance with France. Now Great Britain is not just at war with the colonies' troops. It is in conflict with one of the most powerful nations in the world.

British leaders decide to gather loyalists to their cause. They believe that the loyalists are most numerous in the south and that the war can be won with loyalist support.

In the winter of 1778 thousands of British soldiers descend on Savannah. You are among the hundreds of militiamen defending the city. You try to make a stand, but you are forced to retreat.

As you flee you come across Major General Benjamin Lincoln. He is commander of the Continental Army's southern forces.

"I am marching to Charleston," he says. "But I've heard rumors of British activity near Beaufort. I need the area secured."

Beaufort, South Carolina, is just north of Savannah, along the coast. Charleston is farther north. It is where Lincoln's main army is gathering. Do you offer to march to Beaufort or continue on to Charleston?

To secure Beaufort, turn to page 74.

To march to Charleston, turn to page 75.

As Major General Lincoln marches north to Charleston, you and about 300 men head to Beaufort. You are under the command of Brigadier General William Moultrie. Upon reaching the small town, you learn that the British have attacked Fort Lyttleton. This fort is on Port Royal Island, just outside of town.

On the morning of February 3 you take a ferry to Port Royal Island. With your forces, you also have three cannons.

"At the center of the island there is a small rise," Moultrie says. "We will face the British there."

Gray's Hill is an open area surrounded by woods. You could place your forces on the hill. Or you could take cover from British fire in the trees. Where do you tell Moultrie that your forces should be positioned?

To set up on the hill, turn to page 77.

To take cover in the woods, turn to page 88.

You continue on to Charleston with Major General Lincoln. He is gathering his forces there. But when you arrive in early February, the city is still unprepared for an attack. The city's garrison is small and supplies are limited.

Back in the summer of 1776 British forces tried to capture the city. Several battles were fought around Charleston, but the colonial defenses held. After the capture of Savannah, Major General Lincoln worries that the British will try once again to capture Charleston.

As preparations are made for the city's defense, militiamen from South and North Carolina gather in Charleston. Among them is Colonel Andrew Pickens.

"We must do something," Pickens tells Lincoln. "The British have taken Augusta, Georgia, emboldening loyalists in the area."

Turn the page.

As the Revolutionary War went on, some of the fighting moved to southern colonies such as South Carolina.

"But the city's defenses are weak," another officer argues. "We can't risk sending troops to Augusta."

Do you offer to join Pickens in attacking the loyalist forces, or do you stay to work on preparations for the defense of Charleston?

To join Pickens, turn to page 79.

To stay in Charleston, turn to page 80.

"Setting the cannons atop the rise will give our artillery a clear view of the battlefield," you say.

Moultrie agrees and orders his forces toward the top of Gray's Hill. Looking across the clearing, you see the British forces gathering near the edge of the woods. They are just out of musket range. Though the British have the advantage of cover, you have more firepower.

"Fire," Moultrie orders.

BOOM! BOOM! BOOM! Cannonballs crash into the ground, sending up explosions of dirt. When the smoke clears you see that the British are advancing. They duck behind trees and bushes. Another round of cannon fire rocks the ground. Redcoats fall and cry out in pain.

Soon the British are within musket range.

Turn the page.

BANG! BANG! BANG! Musket balls scream angrily through the air. The soldier next to you falls to the ground. British soldiers drop in front of you. You reload your musket. The sounds of cannon fire and muskets mix with the screams of the injured and dying.

"We are running low on ammunition," someone shouts.

You feel the confidence of the men around you wavering. Just as Moultrie is about to sound the retreat, the British start falling back.

"We've got them on the run!" you shout.

The men cheer. Your small group has just won the Battle of Beaufort. Afterward, Moultrie leads you to Charleston.

Turn to page 80.

Early in February you leave Charleston with Colonel Pickens and about 250 militiamen. You meet up with Colonel John Dooly near the Georgia border. Joining forces nearly doubles your troops.

You cross the Savannah River south of Augusta. There you find a small group of British soldiers. You chase them to Carr's Fort. As they barricade themselves inside the outpost, they leave behind their horses and supplies. Soon after, your scouts learn of a loyalist force marching to Augusta.

"The British will surrender soon," Dooly says. "And then we can take control of the fort."

"By then the loyalists will have reached Augusta," Pickens argues. "We won't be able to risk attacking them then."

What action do you recommend to the officers?

To pursue the loyalists, turn to page 82.

To continue the siege, turn to page 90.

As winter turns to spring, militiamen begin gathering in Charleston. Your forces now number several thousand. The city also receives more supplies and ammunition.

Late in the summer of 1779 French ships sail into Charleston's harbor. They further bolster your forces. With the reinforcements Major General Lincoln decides to go on the offensive. He and the commander of the French force make plans to retake Savannah. You remain behind with a couple thousand troops to defend Charleston.

Continental forces arrive in Georgia in mid-September. The fighting is fierce around Savannah. Colonial forces suffer more than 1,000 casualties in their defeat.

Around mid-October Major General Lincoln returns to Charleston with his remaining troops.

Fierce Revolutionary War battles in the southern states often weakened the British Army even when they were victorious.

"We need to prepare our defense," he tells his troops. "The British will march on Charleston once they receive reinforcements from up north."

You could continue to stay in Charleston. Or you could join General Isaac Huger to help defend Monck's Corner just north of Charleston. How do you offer to help the defense of Charleston?

To defend Monck's Corner, turn to page 85.

To defend Charleston, turn to page 91.

"We need to stop the loyalists," you say.

"I agree," Pickens says. "We can't let them sway others."

You turn your attention from the fort to pursue the loyalist forces across Georgia. You catch them by surprise as they camp near Kettle Creek. Pickens leads the attack on the loyalists. You fight by his side. Dooly flanks him on the right and another officer leads troops on the left.

As you march forward you see a small group of loyalists preparing a defense. The soldiers duck behind some fallen trees.

"Fire!" Pickens orders.

You raise your musket and fire without even taking aim. The idea is not to hit a specific target but to fire as many shots as fast as you can. You reload your musket and fire again seconds later.

During the initial volleys, the loyalists' commander is wounded. Their troops are shaken and start to pull back.

"Charge!" Pickens commands.

Your forces surround the loyalist camp and begin firing. A group of loyalists retreats across the Kettle River. The soldiers try to regroup, but you keep the pressure on them. They continue to fall back as you continue to fire on them.

You know the battle is won when a large group of loyalists surrenders to you. Your victory at the Battle of Kettle Creek disrupts the British recruitment of loyalists. But the coming months are difficult for Continental forces. Major General Lincoln launches a failed attempt to capture Savannah. During the spring of 1780 British forces lay siege to Charleston. When Major General Lincoln is forced to surrender, nearly 5,000 troops are taken prisoner.

Turn the page.

This is the greatest defeat of the Continental Army during the war. Continental forces are sent into disarray and suffer several more losses in the coming months.

Then in January 1781 you again find yourself serving under Colonel Pickens. He is in command of a group of militiamen patrolling along South Carolina's northern border. On the night of the January 16 he joins your force with Brigadier General Daniel Morgan's.

"British forces are gathering behind us," one of Morgan's officers says. "And we have already lost too many troops at Charleston."

"But if we continue to retreat," Pickens argues, "South Carolina will be lost."

Brigadier General Morgan turns to you. "Do you have a suggestion?"

To stay and fight, turn to page 93.

To retreat into North Carolina, turn to page 95.

You march to Monck's Corner with a force of about 500 militiamen. The small town is just north of Charleston.

In the spring of 1780 you hear news that British forces are sailing toward Charleston. They land south of the city and march north.

In early April the British reach Charleston. Their warships sail into Charleston Harbor. British troops take up positions south of the city. But supplies and reinforcements continue to reach Charleston from the north.

Early on the morning of April 14 you wake to musket fire. You jump out of bed and grab your gear.

"We are under attack!" someone shouts.

As you step outside you hear the thump of hooves pounding your way. One of your officers is approaching.

Turn the page.

"Loyalist forces are attacking," he says. "Their numbers are too great."

The retreat begins. As you flee, you hear musket fire ring out along with the commands of British officers.

You are forced to flee north, away from Charleston. With your defeat the British now have Charleston completely surrounded. Within a month Major General Lincoln surrenders. Thousands within the city are taken prisoner. The Continental Army is in disarray.

You flee into North Carolina. The next few months are difficult for the Continental Army. Major General Horatio Gates takes command of the southern forces. But he suffers a major defeat at the Battle of Camden. Loyalist forces in the Carolinas grow stronger. If they continue to strengthen, they could march on Virginia, taking the fight deeper into colonial territory.

Nathaniel Greene takes control of the southern Continental Army. You are placed under the command of Colonel William Campbell. There are rumors of a British force in western North Carolina near the border with South Carolina. It is calling loyalists to arms. Campbell moves his forces to confront the loyalists. They retreat across the border into South Carolina.

"We can't risk pursuing them," an officer argues. "The British control most of South Carolina."

"But we have the loyalists on the run," another officer says.

What action do you recommend to Colonel Campbell?

To hold your position, turn to page 97.

To pursue the loyalists, turn to page 98.

Since most of your forces are poorly trained militiamen, you suggest taking cover in the woods.

"We'll be better protected in the trees," you say.

"But then we will not be able to position our cannons so they have a clear shot at the battlefield," Moultrie says.

He has your forces set up atop Gray's Hill. From there you see the British forces gathering near the edge of the woods. They are just out of musket range. Moultrie orders the cannons to fire.

The British advance, sticking to the cover of trees and brush. You form your battle lines and exchange musket fire with the British.

Musket balls scream through the air. Cannons boom, and cannonballs thud into the ground.

You reload your musket and send another volley into the British lines. Then they return fire. A musket ball slams into your gut.

89

As the battle rages on, you collapse to the ground. While you do not survive the battle, the colonial forces are victorious.

THE END

To follow another path, turn to page 15.
To read the conclusion, turn to page 101.

"Let's capture the fort," you say. "We can use it as a base to launch further attacks."

You have plenty of food in addition to the supplies the British left outside the fort. You do not expect the siege to last long. But Pickens refuses to let go of the idea of the loyalists reaching Augusta.

"We cannot let them get to Augusta," he says. "I am taking my forces to pursue the loyalists."

He leaves you with a small force. You maintain the siege of the fort. But two days later a large force of British troops marches on your location. You are now trapped.

90

You surrender. Your entire force is taken prisoner and forced to march to Savannah with the British troops. As a prisoner of war, your role in the fighting is now over.

THE END

To follow another path, turn to page 15.
To read the conclusion, turn to page 101.

You stay and join the garrison in Charleston after Major General Lincoln's return.

In the spring of 1780 you hear that British forces are sailing toward Charleston. They land south of the city and march north, arriving at the beginning of April.

You have had a year to prepare the city's defenses. You are confident you can hold off a British attack. But instead of attacking, the British slowly circle the city. Their warships sail into Charleston Harbor. Then you hear news of forts around the city falling one by one.

By the beginning of May the city is completely surrounded. That is when the British commander calls for your surrender. At first Major General Lincoln vows to continue fighting. But then the British bombard the city. Not only are your troops in danger but the citizens of Charleston are threatened.

Turn the page.

The British Navy met fierce resistance in South Carolina during the Revolutionary War.

On May 12, 1781, Major General Lincoln surrenders. Several thousand colonial soldiers are taken prisoner. It is the worst defeat suffered by the Continental Army, and its forces in the south are in disarray.

You are among those taken prisoner. Your fight is now over.

THE END

To follow another path, turn to page 15.
To read the conclusion, turn to page 101.

"If we retreat, South Carolina will be lost," you say. "And no one will be left to defend the colonists here."

Brigadier General Morgan agrees with you.

He has you prepare for battle in an area called Hannah's Cowpens. Early the next morning you and Pickens are stationed toward the front of your forces. You defend a small rise. To one side of you lies a ravine and to the other side is a creek. So when the British attack, they must face you head on.

Just before sunrise the British step out of the surrounding woods. They march toward your location.

"Hold your line until I signal the retreat," Pickens commands.

You raise your musket as the enemy approaches.

"Fire!" Pickens orders.

Turn the page.

BANG! BANG! BANG! Shots ring out. You see Redcoats drop in front of you. You reload and send another volley into their lines.

"Retreat!" Pickens calls out.

You dash around the small rise. The British forces break formation and charge straight ahead, hoping for an easy victory. But they don't see the line of Continental soldiers waiting on the other side of the hill. As Redcoats crest the rise, shots ring out. Musket fire shreds the advancing British forces. They are forced to retreat.

Your victory at the Battle of Cowpens is seen as one of the turning points in the Revolutionary War. You hand the British a major defeat while continuing to hold territory in South Carolina. Because of your successes, the Continental Army can continue the fight for independence.

THE END

To follow another path, turn to page 15.
To read the conclusion, turn to page 101.

94

"Let's save our forces to fight another day," you say.

Morgan shakes his head in thought. "It is time we make a stand, or this war will be lost."

He has you prepare for battle at Hannah's Cowpens. You and Pickens are positioned in front of a small rise. Just before sunrise the British march toward your location.

"We will fire two volleys and then retreat," Pickens says before giving the command to fire.

Shots ring out. You see Redcoats drop in front of you. Then they return fire. Musket balls cut through your lines. You feel a pain, like a hammer slamming into your thigh. You crumple to the ground. The troops around you fire another volley. Then Pickens calls for a retreat. Two of your fellow soldiers drag you with them.

95

Turn the page.

The British pursue you. They break formation and charge, thinking they have a victory. But what they do not realize is that more Continental soldiers are waiting on the other side of the hill.

As the British reach the top of the hill, shots ring out. Musket fire rips through the advancing British. They suffer heavy losses and are forced to retreat. The victory at the Battle of Cowpens is a major turning point in the Revolutionary War. It is the British Army's first major defeat in months.

While the Continental Army continues its fight, you are fighting for your life. You suffered a serious injury and your injured leg cannot be fixed. Surgeons have to amputate it. Your time serving in the Continental Army is over.

96

THE END

To follow another path, turn to page 15.
To read the conclusion, turn to page 101.

"It is too dangerous," you say. "We can't risk crossing the border."

Colonel Campbell considers this. "I don't think this is the time to play it safe," he says. "We are too close to catching the loyalist forces."

Campbell has his forces cross into South Carolina. Near a rocky ridge called Kings Mountain, you catch the loyalists by surprise and fire on them from the cover of trees and rocks. A group of loyalists charges down the ridge toward you. The fighting is fierce. Men fall dead or injured on both sides.

As the loyalists start to fall back, you step out from behind your cover to pursue them. You fire a volley into the group and watch as some soldiers drop. You are busy reloading your weapon when a musket ball slams into you, ending your life.

THE END

To follow another path, turn to page 15.
To read the conclusion, turn to page 101.

"We should attack," you say, "before their forces can grow any stronger."

Campbell agrees. He has you cross into South Carolina near a rocky ridge called Kings Mountain. The loyalist forces are unaware of your approach. When you have their camp surrounded, Campbell orders an attack. From the cover of trees and rocks you rain down musket fire on the loyalist forces.

The battles of Kings Mountain and Cowpens were important American victories in the Revolutionary War in the southern states.

A group of loyalists charges down the ridge wielding bayonets. The men around you turn to flee because they do not have bayonets.

"Hold your lines!" Campbell shouts, rallying the troops.

You fire at the loyalists. Many of them falter and fall to the ground. You reload and fire again. More drop, dead and dying. The loyalists are taking heavy losses, and then their leader falls. Soon after, they raise white flags of surrender.

You win the day, defeating a large force of loyalists. The victory at Kings Mountain turns out to be a pivotal battle for the Continental forces. It helps put an end to the British recruitment of loyalists, giving the Continental Army an advantage in the Revolutionary War.

THE END

To follow another path, turn to page 15.
To read the conclusion, turn to page 101.

By the UNITED STATES in CONGRESS Aſſembled,

A PROCLAMATION.

WHEREAS definitive articles of peace and friendſhip, between the United States of America and his Britannic majeſty, were concluded and ſigned at Paris, on the 3d day of September, 1783, by the plenipotentiaries of the ſaid United States, and of his ſaid Britannic Majeſty, duly and reſpectively authorized for that purpoſe; which definitive articles are in the words following.

In the Name of the Moſt Holy and Undivided TRINITY.

IT having pleaſed the Divine Providence to diſpoſe the hearts of the moſt ſerene and moſt potent Prince George the Third, by the Grace of God, King of Great-Britain, France and Ireland, Defender of the Faith, Duke of Brunſwick and Luneaburg, Arch-Treaſurer and Prince Elector of the Holy Roman Empire, &c. and of the United States of America, to forget all paſt miſunderſtandings and differences, that have unhappily interrupted the good correſpondence and friendſhip which they mutually wiſh to reſtore; and to eſtabliſh ſuch a beneficial and ſatisfactory intercourſe between the two countries, upon the ground of reciprocal advantages and mutual convenience, as may promote and ſecure to both perpetual peace and harmony: And having for this deſirable end, already laid the foundation of peace and reconciliation, by the proviſional articles, ſigned at Paris, on the 30th of November, 1782, by the commiſſioners empowered on each part, which articles were agreed to be inſerted in, and to conſtitute the treaty of peace propoſed to be concluded between the crown of Great-Britain and the ſaid United States, but which treaty was not to be concluded until terms of peace ſhould be agreed upon between Great-Britain and France, and his Britannic majeſty ſhould be ready to conclude ſuch treaty accordingly; and the treaty between Great-Britain and France, having ſince been concluded, his Britannic majeſty and the United States of America, in order to carry into full effect the proviſional articles abovementioned, according to the tenor thereof, have conſtituted and appointed, that is to ſay, His Britannic majeſty on his part, David Hartley, eſquire, member of the parliament of Great-Britain, and the ſaid United States on their part, John Adams, eſquire, late a commiſſioner of the United States of America at the court of Verſailles, late delegate in congreſs from the ſtate of Maſſachuſetts, and chief juſtice of the ſaid ſtate, and miniſter plenipotentiary of the ſaid United States, to their high mightineſſes the States General of the United Netherlands; Benjamin Franklin, eſquire, late delegate in congreſs from the ſtate of Pennſylvania, preſident of the convention of the ſaid ſtate, and miniſter plenipotentiary from the United States of America at the court of Verſailles; John Jay, eſquire, late preſident of congreſs, and chief juſtice of the ſtate of New-York, and miniſter plenipotentiary from the ſaid United States at the Court of Madrid, to be the plenipotentiaries for the concluding and ſigning the preſent definitive treaty, who after having reciprocally communicated their reſpective full powers, have agreed upon and confirmed the following articles.

ARTICLE 1ſt. His Britannic Majeſty acknowledges the ſaid United States, viz. New-Hampſhire, Maſſachuſetts-Bay, Rhode-Iſland and Providence Plantations, Connecticut, New-York, New-Jerſey, Pennſylvania, Delaware, Maryland, Virginia, North-Carolina, South-Carolina and Georgia, to be free, ſovereign and independent ſtates; that he treats with them as ſuch, and for himſelf, his heirs and ſucceſſors, relinquiſhes all claims to the government, propriety and territorial rights of the ſame, and every part thereof:

ARTICLE. 2d. And that all diſputes which might ariſe in future on the ſubject of the boundaries of the ſaid United States may be prevented, it is hereby agreed and declared, that the following are and ſhall be their boundaries, viz.

From the north weſt angle of Nova-Scotia, viz. that angle which is formed by a line drawn due north from the ſource of Saint-Croix river to the Highlands; along the ſaid Highlands which divide thoſe rivers that empty themſelves into the river Saint Lawrence from thoſe which fall into the Atlantic Ocean, to the north-weſternmoſt head of Connecticut river, thence down along the middle of that river to the forty-fifth degree of north latitude; from thence by a line due weſt on ſaid latitude, until it ſtrikes the river Iroquois or Cataraquy; thence along the middle of ſaid river into lake Ontario, through the middle of ſaid lake until it ſtrikes the communication by water between that lake and lake Erie; thence along the middle of ſaid communication into lake Erie, through the middle of ſaid lake until it arrives at the water communication between that lake and lake Huron; thence along the middle of ſaid water communication into the lake Huron; thence through the middle of ſaid lake to the water communication between that lake and lake Superior; thence through lake Superior northward of the iſles, Royal and Philipeaux to the long lake; thence through the middle of ſaid long lake and the water communication between it and the lake of the Woods, to the ſaid lake of the Woods; thence through the ſaid lake to the moſt north-weſtern point thereof, and from thence on a due weſt courſe to the river Miſſiſippi; thence by a line to be drawn along the middle of the ſaid river Miſſiſippi, until it ſhall interſect the northernmoſt part of the thirty-firſt degree of north latitude. South by a line to be drawn due eaſt from the determination of the line laſt mentioned, in the latitude of thirty-one degrees north of the equator, to the middle of the river Apalachicola or Catahouche; thence along the middle thereof to its junction with the Flint river; thence ſtraight to the head of Saint Mary's river; and thence down along the middle of Saint Mary's river to the Atlantic Ocean. Eaſt by a line to be drawn along the middle of the river Saint-Croix, from its mouth in the bay of Fundy to its ſource, and from its ſource directly north to the aforeſaid Highlands which divide the rivers that fall into the Atlantic Ocean from thoſe which fall into the river Saint Lawrence; comprehending all iſlands within twenty leagues of any part of the ſhores of the United States, and lying between lines to be drawn due eaſt from the points where the aforeſaid boundaries between Nova-Scotia on the one part, and Eaſt Florida on the other, ſhall reſpectively touch the bay of Fundy, and the Atlantic Ocean; excepting ſuch iſlands as now are or heretofore have been within the limits of the ſaid province of Nova Scotia.

ARTICLE. 3d. It is agreed that the people of the United States ſhall continue to enjoy unmoleſted the right to take fiſh of every kind on the Grand Bank, and on all the other banks of Newfoundland; alſo in the gulph of Saint Lawrence, and at all other places in the ſea, where the inhabitants of both countries uſed at any time heretofore to fiſh; and alſo that the inhabitants of the United States ſhall have liberty to take fiſh of every kind on ſuch part of the coaſt of Newfoundland as Britiſh fiſhermen ſhall uſe, (but not to dry or cure the ſame on that Iſland) and alſo on the coaſts, bays and creeks of all other of his Britannic Majeſty's dominions in America; and that the American fiſhermen ſhall have liberty to dry and cure fiſh in any of the unſettled bays, harbours and creeks of Nova-Scotia, Magdalen iſlands, and Labradore, ſo long as the ſame ſhall remain unſettled, but ſo ſoon as the ſame or either of them ſhall be ſettled, it ſhall not be lawful for the ſaid fiſhermen to dry or cure fiſh at ſuch ſettlement, without a previous agreement for that purpoſe with the inhabitants, proprietors or poſſeſſors of the ground.

ARTICLE 4th. It is agreed that creditors on either ſide, ſhall meet with no lawful impediment to the recovery of the full value in ſterling money, of all bona fide debts heretofore contracted.

ARTICLE 5th. It is agreed that the Congreſs ſhall earneſtly recommend it to the legiſlatures of the reſpective ſtates, to provide for the reſtitution of all eſtates, rights and properties, which have been confiſcated, belonging to real Britiſh ſubjects, and alſo of the eſtates, rights and properties of perſons reſident in diſtricts in the poſſeſſion of his majeſty's arms, and who have not borne arms againſt the ſaid United States. And that perſons of any other deſcription ſhall have free liberty to go to any part or parts of any of the Thirteen United States, and therein to remain twelve months unmoleſted in their endeavours to obtain the reſtitution of ſuch of their eſtates, rights and properties, as may have been confiſcated; and that Congreſs ſhall alſo earneſtly recommend to the ſeveral ſtates a reconſideration and reviſion of all acts or laws regarding the premiſes, ſo as to render the ſaid laws or acts perfectly conſiſtent, not only with juſtice and equity, but with that ſpirit of conciliation, which on the return of the bleſſings of peace ſhould univerſally prevail. And that Congreſs ſhall alſo earneſtly recommend to the ſeveral ſtates, that the eſtates, rights and properties of ſuch laſt mentioned perſons ſhall be reſtored to them; they refunding to any perſons who may be now in poſſeſſion the bona fide price (where any has been given) which ſuch perſons may have paid on purchaſing any of the ſaid lands, rights or properties ſince the confiſcation. And it is agreed that all perſons who have any intereſt in confiſcated lands, either by debts, marriage ſettlements, or otherwiſe, ſhall meet with no lawful impediment in the proſecution of their juſt rights.

ARTICLE 6th. That there ſhall be no future confiſcations made, nor any proſecutions commenced againſt any perſon or perſons for or by reaſon of the part which he or they may have taken in the preſent war; and that no perſon ſhall on that account, ſuffer any future loſs or damage, either in his perſon liberty or property, and that thoſe who may be in confinement on ſuch charges, at the time of the ratification of the treaty in America, ſhall be immediately ſet at liberty, and the proſecutions ſo commenced be diſcontinued.

ARTICLE 7th. There ſhall be a firm and perpetual peace between his Britannic Majeſty and the ſaid States, and between the ſubjects of the one, and the citizens of the other, wherefore all hoſtilities both by ſea and land ſhall from henceforth ceaſe: all priſoners on both ſides ſhall be ſet at liberty, and his Britannic Majeſty ſhall with all convenient ſpeed, and without cauſing any deſtruction, or carrying away any negroes or other property of the American inhabitants, withdraw all his armies, garriſons and fleets from the ſaid United States, and from every poſt place and harbour within the ſame; leaving in all fortifications the American artillery that may be therein, and ſhall alſo order and cauſe all archives, records deeds and papers, belonging to any of the ſaid ſtates, or their citizens, which in the courſe of the war may have fallen into the hands of his officers, to be forthwith reſtored and delivered to the proper ſtates and perſons to whom they belong.

ARTICLE 8th. The navigation of the river Miſſiſippi, from its ſource to the Ocean, ſhall forever remain free and open to the ſubjects of Great-Britain and the citizens of the United States.

ARTICLE 9th. In caſe it ſhould ſo happen that any place or territory belonging to Great-Britain or to the United States, ſhould have been conquered by the arms of either from the other, before the arrival of the ſaid proviſional articles in America, it is agreed, that the ſame ſhall be reſtored without difficulty, and without requiring any compenſation.

ARTICLE 10th. The ſolemn ratifications of the preſent treaty, expedited in good and due form, ſhall be exchanged between the contracting parties, in the ſpace of ſix months, or ſooner if poſſible, to be computed from the day of the ſignature of the preſent treaty. In witneſs whereof, we the underſigned, their miniſters plenipotentiary, have in their name and in virtue of our full powers, ſigned with our hands the preſent definitive treaty, and, cauſed the ſeals of our arms to be affixed thereto.

DONE at Paris, this third day of September, in the year of our Lord one thouſand ſeven hundred and eighty-three.

(L. S.) D. HARTLEY, (L. S.) JOHN ADAMS,
(L. S.) B. FRANKLIN,
(L. S.) JOHN JAY.

AND we the United States in Congreſs aſſembled, having ſeen and duly conſidered the definitive articles aforeſaid, did by a certain act under the ſeal of the United States, bearing date this 14th day of January 1784, approve, ratify and confirm the ſame and every part and clauſe thereof, engaging and promiſing that we would ſincerely and faithfully perform and obſerve the ſame, and never ſuffer them to be violated by any one, or tranſgreſſed in any manner as far as ſhould be in our power: and being ſincerely diſpoſed to carry the ſaid articles into execution truly, honeſtly and with good faith, according to the intent and meaning thereof, we have thought proper by theſe preſents, to notify the premiſes to all the good citizens of theſe United States, hereby requiring and enjoining all bodies of magiſtracy, legiſlative, executive and judiciary, all perſons bearing office, civil or military, of whatever rank, degree or powers, and all others the good citizens of theſe States of every vocation and condition, that reverencing thoſe ſtipulations entered into on their behalf, under the authority of that fœderal bond by which their exiſtence as an independent people is bound up together, and is known and acknowledged by the nations of the world, and with that good faith which is every man's ſureſt guide within their ſeveral offices juriſdictions and vocations, they carry into effect the ſaid definitive articles, and every clauſe and ſentence thereof, ſincerely, ſtrictly and completely.

GIVEN under the Seal of the United States, Witneſs his Excellency THOMAS MIFFLIN, our Preſident, at Annapolis, this fourteenth day of January, in the year of our Lord one thouſand ſeven hundred and eighty-four, and of the ſovereignty and independence of the United States of America the eighth.

Cha Thomson

ANNAPOLIS: Printed by JOHN DUNLAP, Printer for the United States in Congreſs aſſembled.

Americans learned that the Treaty of Paris had been ratified when Congress released an official proclamation.

CHAPTER 5

A NEW NATION

The American Revolution would not officially be over until a treaty was signed.

Early in 1782 John Adams, Benjamin Franklin, and John Jay sailed to Paris. There the French oversaw negotiations with British officials. Not every issue between the United States and Great Britain was resolved. But these three Founding Fathers helped achieve two important goals. First, the British agreed to recognize the United States of America as an independent nation. Second, the new nation acquired all of the land east of the Mississippi River. This new territory nearly doubled the size of the United States. The Treaty of Paris was signed on September 3, 1783.

Now that their independence was won, the difficult work began. The Founding Fathers needed to build a new nation from a war-torn country. Lawmakers had to decide upon the laws that would govern the people of the United States. They laid the foundation of this new government in the U.S. Constitution.

Once the Constitution was written, each of the 13 states voted on whether to ratify it. Nine states needed to approve the Constitution for it to become law. That happened on June 21, 1788, when New Hampshire approved the Constitution. This document then became the law of the land starting March 4, 1789.

The Constitution said that a president would oversee the government's executive branch. General George Washington was a hero of the Revolutionary War and he was elected the country's first president. He served two terms.

Other Founding Fathers, such as Thomas Jefferson and John Adams, also served as president.

As the people of the United States learned how to govern themselves, the people of France rebelled against the rule of their monarch, Louis XVI. Helping the United States gain its independence had helped cause a financial crisis in France. Unfair taxes also led to people suffering many hardships. The French Revolution began in the spring of 1789. Fighting engulfed much of Europe as Great Britain and other countries tried to quell the rebellion.

103

The French revolutionaries asked for aid from the United States. There were some in the U.S. government who wanted to help. The French people had helped the colonists fight for their independence. Others wanted to side with the British. They still felt loyal to Great Britain.

The Treaty of Ghent was a peace treaty ending the War of 1812. It was signed on December 24, 1814.

But Washington managed to keep the country neutral in the overseas conflict. The new nation did not have the resources to enter another war.

The United States' neutrality came at a cost. Both France and Great Britain imposed economic penalties. The British attacked U.S. merchant ships and armed American Indians who were in conflict with the United States.

Eventually U.S. lawmakers could not ignore the British actions against their sovereignty. About 30 years after the end of the Revolutionary War, the United States declared war on Great Britain.

Known as the War of 1812, this new conflict helped resolve issues left over from the American Revolution. Neither side could claim victory. But with the end of the war, the British stopped blocking Americans from trading with other nations. They also stopped supporting American Indians in their conflicts with the United States. Most importantly, the United States had held its own against Great Britain. This instilled confidence in the citizens as they continued the work of building a new nation.

TIMELINE

April 19, 1775—Battles of Lexington and Concord; colonial militiamen force the British to retreat to Boston

May 10, 1775—Capture of Fort Ticonderoga; colonists capture fort and its artillery

May 10, 1775—Second Continental Congress is established to govern the colonies during their fight for freedom

June 14, 1775—Second Continental Congress selects General George Washington to lead the newly formed Continental Army

June 17, 1775—Battle of Bunker (Breed's) Hill; British drive colonial forces from the Charlestown Peninsula, but the Redcoats suffer heavy losses, helping build American confidence in their ability to fight the British

March 17, 1776—British leave Boston and sail to Halifax

July 4, 1776—Official adoption of the Declaration of Independence

August 27, 1776—Battle of Long Island, also known as the Battle of Brooklyn Heights; British force the Continental Army to retreat north onto Manhattan

October 28, 1776—Battle of White Plains; British victory

December 26, 1776—Battle of Trenton; colonial victory

January 3, 1777—Battle of Princeton; colonial victory

September 11, 1777—Battle of Brandywine; British victory

February 6, 1778—Treaties of Alliance and of Amity and Commerce are signed with the French

December 29, 1778—British capture Savannah, Georgia

February 3, 1779—Battle of Beaufort, also known as Battle of Port Royal Island; colonial victory

February 14, 1779—Battle of Kettle Creek; colonial victory

April 2, 1780—Siege of Charleston begins; colonists suffer the worst defeat of the war

April 14, 1780—Battle of Monck's Corner; British victory

August 16, 1780—Battle of Camden; British victory

October 7, 1780—Battle of Kings Mountain; colonial victory puts an end to the loyalist powers

January 17, 1981—Battle of Cowpens; colonial victory

October 9, 1781—Battle of Yorktown; British surrender

September 3, 1783—Treaty of Paris is signed, officially ending the Revolutionary War

March 4, 1789—George Washington begins serving his first term as U.S. president

OTHER PATHS TO EXPLORE

In this book, you've seen how events from the past look different from three points of view. Perspectives on history are as varied as the people who lived it. Seeing history from many points of view is an important part of understanding it. Here are ideas for other Revolutionary War points of view to explore.

+ Not everyone had confidence in General George Washington's ability to command the Continental Army. Some members of the Second Continental Congress and the military wanted to replace him, especially after his defeats in New York. Using other texts or valid Internet sources, research some of the arguments for and against keeping Washington as commander of the army.

+ Although the colonies needed support from France, some members of Congress worried about France's influence over the United States of America once the war was over. How might things have turned out differently if the French had kept their forces in the United States after the war ended?

READ MORE

Doeden, Matt. *Weapons of the Revolutionary War.* North Mankato, Minn.: Capstone Press, 2018.

Hinman, Bonnie. *The Second Continental Congress.* Hallandale, Fla.: Mitchell Lane Publishers, 2018.

Marciniak, Kristin. *The Revolutionary War: Why They Fought.* North Mankato, Minn.: Compass Point Books, 2016.

Nagle, Jeanne. *How George Washington Fought the Revolutionary War.* New York: Enslow Publishing, 2018.

INTERNET SITES

Use FactHound to find Internet sites related to this book.

Visit *www.facthound.com*

Just type in 9781543515404 and go.

GLOSSARY

alliance (uh-LY-uhnts)—an agreement between nations or groups of people to work together

artillery (ar-TIL-uh-ree)—cannons and other large guns used during battles

bayonet (BAY-uh-net)—a long metal blade attached to the end of a musket or rifle

casualty (KAZH-oo-uhl-tee)—a person killed, wounded, or missing in a battle or in a war

garrison (GA-ruh-suhn)—a group of soldiers based in a town or fort and ready to defend it

loyalist (LOI-uh-list)—a colonist who was loyal to Great Britain during the Revolutionary War

militia (muh-LISH-uh)—group of volunteer citizens organized to fight, but who are not professional soldiers

morale (muh-RAL)—the feelings of a group or person

Parliament (PAR-luh-muhnt)—the national legislature of Great Britain

patriot (PAY-tree-uht)—a person who sided with the colonies during the Revolutionary War

ratify (RAT-uh-fie)—formally approve

siege (SEEJ)—an attack designed to surround a place and cut it off from supplies or help

surrender (suh-REN-dur)—to give up or admit defeat in battle

BIBLIOGRAPHY

Carp, Benjamin. *Defiance of the Patriots*. New Haven, Conn.: Yale University Press, 2010.

Ellis, Joseph J. *American Creation: Triumphs and Tragedies at the Founding of the Republic*. New York: A. A. Knopf, 2007.

Fischer, David Hackett. *Washington's Crossing*. New York: Oxford University Press, 2004.

Forbes, Esther. *Paul Revere and the World He Lived In*. Boston: Houghton Mifflin, 1988.

Gross, Robert A. *The Minutemen and Their World*. New York: Hill and Wang, 2001.

Wood, Gordon S. *The American Revolution: A History*. New York: Modern Library, 2002.

INDEX